Atlantic Bottlenose Dolphin

Blue Whale

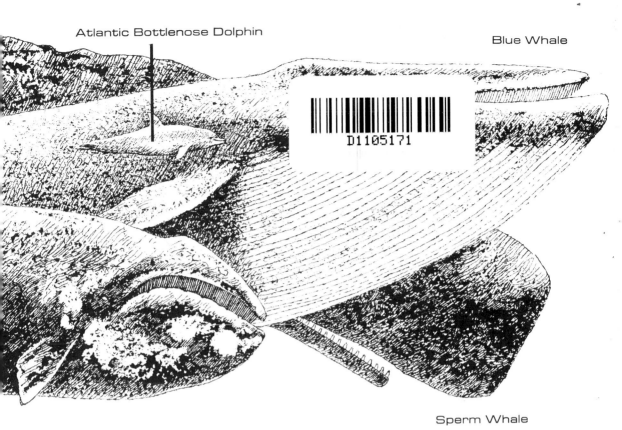

Sperm Whale

Narwhal

Killer Whale

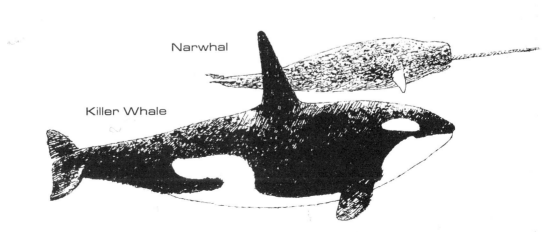

Whales:

Their Life in the Sea

Narwhal

Whales:

Their Life in the Sea

by Faith McNulty

Illustrations by John Schoenherr

Harper & Row, Publishers
New York, Evanston, San Francisco, London

WHALES: THEIR LIFE IN THE SEA
Text copyright © 1975 by Faith McNulty
Illustrations copyright © 1975 by John Schoenherr
Library of Congress Catalog Card Number: 74–20395
Trade Standard Book Number: 06–024168–3
Harpercrest Standard Book Number: 06–024169–1

FIRST EDITION

To "whale people" everywhere
who are working for a new era of
amnesty, mercy, and scientific understanding

Contents

Pacific White-sided Dolphin

Chapter One
Introducing Whales

Gray Whale

Chapter One
Introducing Whales

Of all the animals on earth, the strangest to us are the great whales. They are huge. They are shaped like fish. They have warm blood and give milk. They breathe air, not water. They spend their lives swimming through cold and trackless oceans. They are man's most mysterious cousins.

Because of their life in the sea, whales are the most difficult of all animals for us to study. And it is even harder for us, who live on land, to imagine what it is like to be a whale—to swim forever, never touching land, diving into dark depths, and coming to the surface only for a breath of air.

Biologists study land animals by watching them as they lead their normal lives. They study what the animal eats, where it goes, how it "talks" to other animals, how it finds a mate and cares for its young.

In the case of whales, such studies are difficult. A swimming whale shows only a small part of its body above water, and then

4

only for a moment as it comes up to breathe. By using diving gear a few men have managed to see wild whales under water. They have even photographed them. But because whales swim so fast, not even divers have been able to stay with whales for very long. Perhaps someday someone will invent a tiny submarine in which a man can join a group of whales, swim with them under the sea, and watch everything they do.

Such an invention would delight biologists, who want very much to know more about the lives of whales, but it doesn't seem likely to happen soon. At the present time we can only imagine what whales do under water; how their huge forms glide swiftly through the shadowy depths; how they plunge into the dark and cold far below; how they find their way by special senses that humans do not have.

Yet, in spite of the difficulties of studying whales, we have found out a surprising number of things about them. Some of this knowledge has come to us through the hunting of whales.

For hundreds of years men have hunted whales in order to make use of their huge bodies. The fat on a whale's body is called blubber. It can be turned into valuable oil. Before electricity was discovered, this oil was used in lamps. Now it is turned into margarine and other products. Oil and margarine are useful things, but they can be gotten from plants as well as from whales. Many people think it is wrong to kill whales when we can get along very well without killing them.

The hunting of whales has been a cruel and bloody story, but from it we have learned a great deal about them. Scientists have cut open dead whales and looked into their enormous insides.

When they examined blue whales, which are the largest species, they found that the arteries through which their blood flows are as big around as stovepipes and that their hearts weigh a thousand pounds.

One of the most interesting discoveries is that whales have very large brains, larger than any other animal. The surface of the whale's brain has many small wrinkles, called convolutions, that we know have something to do with the ability to think. Biologists believe that whales are very intelligent animals.

Other scientists have studied the sounds that whales make under water. They have discovered that each kind of whale makes a different sort of sound, and that whales' voices travel many miles through the water. To our ears these sounds are strange and eerie and even beautiful. Some can be called songs.

We have also learned something about where whales go and what they do at various times of the year. Whales are found in all the oceans of the world. Some make long journeys, called migrations, as the seasons change. The large whales swim all the way from the cold waters of the North Pole and the South Pole to the warm waters near the midline of the earth, a region called the equator, where it is warm all the year round. Even though the oceans across which they swim are vast, and seem to us to have few landmarks, the whales somehow know where they are going. Each year they can be found at the same place at the same time.

When we think of whales, we think of them as being found only in the deepest ocean, but in fact whales often come close to land. In early times even large whales were a common sight in waters close to the United States. On the East Coast they traveled along the New England shores. The early settlers killed them year after year until at last no more whales appeared. The few of their kind that remain in the Atlantic no longer come close to our shores, but can be found farther out to sea.

On the California coast, where thousands of large whales migrated close to shore, they were also killed. Luckily a few hundred escaped. They have again increased in number, and now many thousands can be seen from shore or from small boats. People gather by the hundreds to see these great beasts go by. Though they are fifty feet long they show only small parts of their bodies when they swim. When they breathe, a spout of water vapor shoots into the air. For watchers on the shore it is a marvelous sight.

There are two very different kinds of whales. Some have teeth with which to catch their food. They do not chew, but swallow food whole. Others have no teeth. Instead, they have an arrangement like a sieve in their mouths where upper teeth would be. It is made of a stuff called baleen. Baleen is tough and flexible, something like the substance fingernails are made of. It grows from the roof of the whale's mouth in fine strips, or plates. Each plate of baleen ends in hairlike fibers. Baleen is rather like the frayed teeth of a comb.

The food of baleen whales consists of tiny bits of life floating and swimming in the water. Some are plants. Some are little animals no bigger than the average insect—small shrimps, for instance, and tiny crablike creatures, and many kinds of newly hatched larvae. Biologists call this mixture of various kinds of small sea life plankton. Plankton does not mean any particular kind of plant or animal. It means whatever is small and alive and drifting in the sea.

When a baleen whale feeds, it takes a great mouthful of water full of plankton. Then it raises its huge tongue and squirts the water out through the baleen the way a person might squirt water through his teeth. The plankton is caught in the baleen. When all the water has drained out, the whale swallows the plankton.

It is one of the marvels of the baleen whales that though they live on the tiniest bits of food they grow to be the biggest animals on earth. At certain times of the year and in certain places, ocean water is so full of plankton that the whales are able to strain out tons of it. Plankton is rich, nourishing food. On this diet the baleen whales are able to grow to tremendous size.

The baleen whales are the huge whales—the Lords of the Sea. The toothed whales are quite different. Although there are several kinds, most of them are small. Small for a whale, that is. Even the smallest of them is as large as a man, and a man is a big animal. Dolphins, whose size averages nine or ten feet, are toothed whales. So are porpoises. Porpoise is simply another name for a certain kind of dolphin. The largest of the dolphin family is the killer whale—a beautiful black-and-white whale, thirty feet long, that is often kept and trained in marine aquariums.

Other kinds of toothed whales are the bottle-nosed whale, which is also about thirty feet long; the beluga or white whale,

which is sixteen feet; and the narwhal, which has a strange, single twisted tusk. Much larger, and quite different from the other toothed whales, is the sperm whale. It is a giant, sixty feet long. It has a huge, square head twenty feet long and nine feet high. There is a famous book called *Moby Dick* that is about a sperm whale.

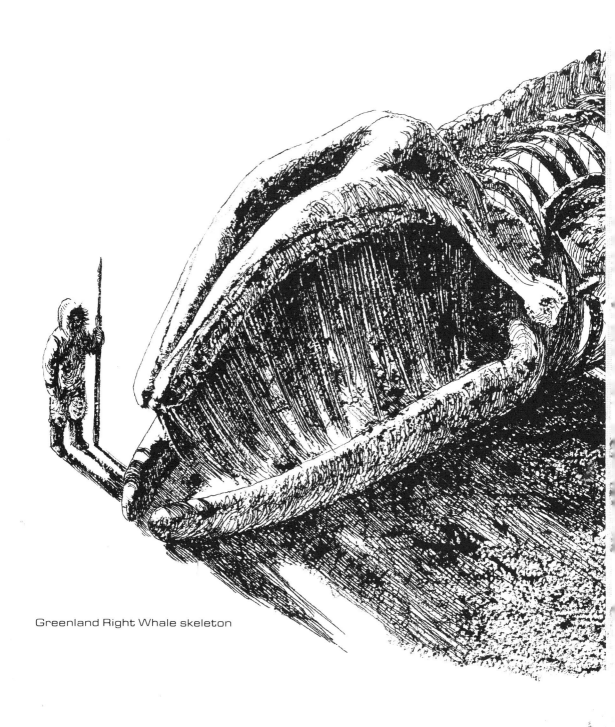

Greenland Right Whale skeleton

Chapter Two
Evolution of Whales

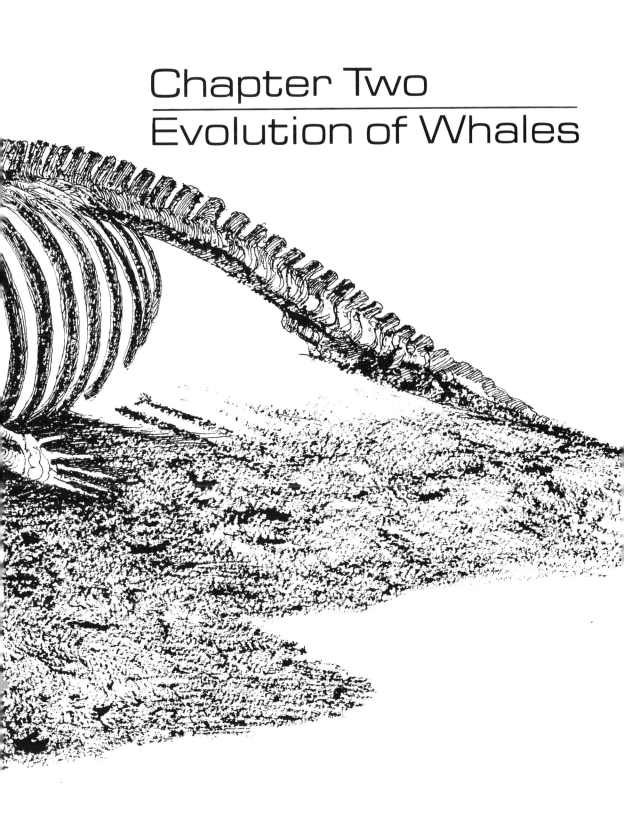

Chapter Two
Evolution of Whales

Whales live only in the water, but they are not fish. Nor are they related to fish. Once, long ago, they were land animals. Their ancestors breathed air and moved about on four legs and then returned to the sea from which all life came.

Fish are much more primitive than whales. We call them "cold-blooded." Their bodies produce no heat. In cold water they are cold. In warm water they are warm. They have gills that take oxygen from the water and cannot take it from air. Their nervous systems are comparatively simple. They are not intelligent in the sense that higher animals are.

Whales, both toothed and baleen, and also mice and men, belong to a great class of creatures called mammals. The word comes from the Latin word for the milk-producing gland by which such animals feed their young. There are about 15,000 species, or kinds, of mammals. On land, they range in size from the tiny shrew, two inches long, to the elephant that stands ten feet tall. Mammals are the highest form of life on earth: that is, the most complicated and intelligent.

Scientists have divided all animals into groups according to how closely they are related. There are large groups called orders. Human beings are in the order of Primates, which also includes apes and monkeys. The whales are in an order known as the Cetacea. The order Cetacea is divided into two suborders. The baleen whales are in the suborder Mysticeti, and the toothed whales are in the suborder Odontoceti.

Each suborder is again divided into smaller groups called families. These include several kinds of whales that are more like each other than like those in other families. Families are divided into genera, and genera are made up of species. A species of animal is one which is by itself. Other species may be closely related, but none is exactly the same. Each species usually mates only with its own kind.

Among the whales there are six families of toothed whales and three families of baleen whales. In most cases each family contains a number of species. These species are different from each other in various ways, but they are all alike in that they are mammals that live in the sea.

The word *whale* may be related to the same ancient word as our word *wheel*. When a whale swims near the surface of the water its shiny, black back surges out of water and seems to revolve like a slowly turning wheel.

It seems strange indeed that an air-breathing, milk-giving, warm-blooded animal lives totally in the sea like a fish. To find an explanation, scientists have examined the bones of whales and compared them with those of other mammals and with the bones of earlier forms of whales that have been found buried in the earth.

Both toothed whales and baleen whales are descended from land animals, but probably from different land animals that returned to the sea at different times. In each case their ancestors were small, hairy creatures with sharp teeth. Those that became the toothed whales seem to have had long tails, while those that turned into baleen whales had short tails. They may have returned to the water at different places and times—perhaps millions of years apart.

The ancestral creatures must have lived on the shore, perhaps where there were gently sloping beaches of sand or mud. They may have fed on small fish and crablike water animals. It is possible to imagine how they began to wade farther and farther into the shallows as they searched for food and then began to swim. They swam, not like fish with fins, but using their tails to push them along. These strange new creatures began to dive, and as the ages passed each generation changed a little and became better suited to the water. They learned to hold their breath longer and longer under water. Finally they no longer came to land at all, and in that way the whales were born.

Meanwhile, on land, other relatives of the same animals that began the whales were developing in still other ways, and became animals with a hoof formed of two toes. Today their descendants include cattle, sheep, goats, pigs, and camels. Although ages of time and slow change separate the whales from the hoofed animals, they are relatives nonetheless.

14

In order to put together a history of prehistoric animals, scientists dig up and examine bones that have been buried in the earth and turned to stone. These ancient bones are called fossils. In the case of whales the fossils that have turned up are few and far between. The bones of the earliest whales, those that are halfway between life on land and life in the sea, have never been found. Possibly this is because they lived along swampy, sandy shores where their bones were lost. Later, when the whales became truly seagoing, their bones sank and were lost in the depths. They can be dug up only in places where the sea has withdrawn and left the old sea beds exposed. However, a few have been found in various parts of the world, especially in Egypt and on the Gulf Coast of the United States.

The earliest fossils of whales that have been found are of those that lived about fifty million years ago. These were not the direct ancestors of today's whales, but were cousins whose line later died out. The bones of the direct ancestor of today's whales are still missing. We can only guess what this primitive whale looked like. From the ancient bones of its relatives we know that there were several kinds of prehistoric whales. One looked like a sea serpent and swam by whipping a long, flexible tail. This early whale had a skull something like that of a dog. Its foreleg had five fingers, but it had no hind legs. Other early whales were like modern porpoises and swam by stroking their tails up and down. Probably no early whales were as large as modern whales.

We can tell how whales have developed not only by looking at the bones of dead whales, but also by examining the bodies of living whales. During their millions of years in the sea they

15

have gradually lost many things that once were useful on land, but became only a hindrance in the water. Whales have lost their fur, outer ears, hind legs, and front toes. Nevertheless, if we look closely we find that traces of all these things remain.

Land animals have bones that form a pelvis to which their hind legs are attached. Whales have no hind legs and no longer need a pelvis, but they still have inside them a small bone that is a relic of the pelvis they had when they walked on four legs.

Like land mammals, the whale begins life as a fertilized egg within a special sac called a uterus in the belly of the female. It has been discovered that as this tiny developing baby, called an embryo, grows larger, it goes through stages in which it resembles its long-dead ancestors. This is true of all mammals. Therefore, by examining whale embryos we gain an idea of the whale's past form. The embryonic whale is shaped very much like other mammal embryos. It looks like the early stages of an unborn pig—or human being, for that matter. It has a round head, a snout, a neck, ridges where ears might grow, and buds where hind legs should be. Usually these tiny hind legs disappear as the embryo develops, but now and then they remain and grow. Then a freak whale is born with partly formed hind legs.

Instead of front legs the whale has two long paddles, called flippers. They are used to steer and balance in the water. The flippers have a perfectly smooth surface, but the bones inside them are almost exactly the same as those in human arms and hands. Most species of whales have five finger bones, though some lack a thumb. The wrist and elbow joints are stiff, but the shoulder joint moves just like our own.

16

Whales breathe through an opening called a blowhole that is on top of the head. It is the first part of the whale to come out of water when it rises from a dive, and allows the whale to take an immediate breath without raising the rest of its head above the surface. In the toothed whales the blowhole is a single opening. In the baleen whales it is double, like our own nostrils.

The embryos of all kinds of whales have two nostrils at the tip of the snout, like any land animal. This changes as the embryo develops. As the head grows larger, the nostrils move toward the top of the head. In this case what happens in a short time in the developing embryo resembles the stages that prehistoric whales went through as they moved from land to the sea.

Greenland Right Whale

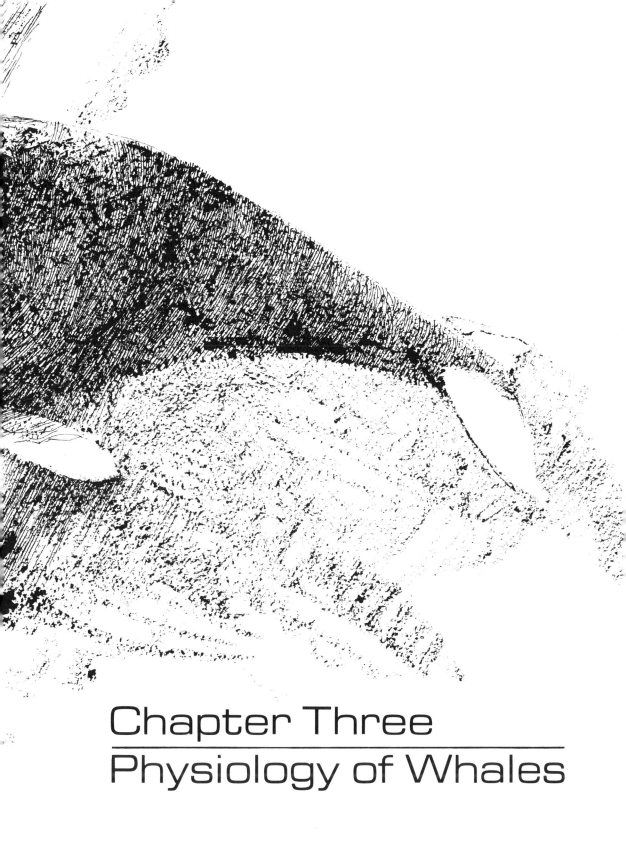

Chapter Three
Physiology of Whales

Chapter Three
Physiology of Whales

Every whale has within its streamlined body all the organs that land animals possess. The blood of a great blue whale, hundreds of gallons of it, is driven through its body by a heart that is six feet across. This huge heart is, nevertheless, in the same proportion to the animal's body weight as the heart of a rabbit is. The whale's stomach has several chambers or compartments, like the stomach of a cow.

The whale's reproductive system is quite like that of other mammals, except that the sex organs that are outside the bodies of land animals are sheathed in the bodies of whales. They are hidden within a slit in the underside of the whale's body. In female whales the mammary glands—the glands that give milk to the young—are also hidden in two smaller slits on either side of the larger slit.

Whales have only one young one at a time, and adult females have only two teats to suckle them; but when the porpoise is in the embryo stage it has eight teats. From this we can guess that long ago it gave birth to litters of young like many land animals.

Whales no longer have hair on their bodies, but there are whiskers on the chin and upper jaw of certain kinds of large whales. These whiskers are not just relics of the past, but seem to serve a purpose. They are surrounded by nerve fibers and probably are organs of touch, like the whiskers of a cat or a dog. With them whales can feel objects immediately in front of them that they cannot see; this must be useful in finding food. Perhaps they tell the whale the speed and direction of water currents flowing by.

Although whales once walked on four legs and are like land animals in many ways, there are also many ways in which they are unlike any other mammal. Size, of course, is the most outstanding thing about a whale. Even a small whale is big compared to most land animals.

The size of animals on land is limited by the amount of weight their legs can carry. This limit was reached by the prehistoric giant reptiles. They grew to weigh thirty or thirty-five tons. Had they grown any bigger they would have been unable to move. Even so, they probably found their huge bodies very cumbersome and spent a great part of their lives partly under water in swamps or shallow lakes. Water supports weight, as anyone can discover by floating in a bathtub. Whales are totally supported by water, and so for them weight is not a problem. That is why whales have been able to grow larger than even the greatest giants of the land.

But even in the sea there is a limit to the size a creature can grow. This comes at the point where its internal organs, such as the heart, the lungs, and the stomach, can no longer supply oxygen and food to such a vast amount of tissue. The largest whales have probably reached this limit.

However, the whale's great size is an advantage in meeting another problem in the sea—that of keeping warm. Heat flows through water more rapidly than it does through air. For this reason a warm-blooded animal loses body warmth more rapidly in the sea than on land. The flow of water past a whale's skin takes away heat just as a breeze chills the naked skin of a human on land. If a whale were very small it would be robbed of its heat faster than it could manufacture it. This is the reason there are no sea mice or sea rabbits. Such small mammals would die of cold. But the whale's huge body can produce a huge amount of heat and so it is able to keep warm.

The streamlined shape of the whale also helps it in its struggle to keep warm. This is because heat is lost through the contact of the water with the skin's surface. An object that is smooth in shape has a smaller surface area than an object the same size with an irregular shape. Streamlining in the whale not only helps it slip through the water more easily, but also reduces heat loss.

As the whale swims through the eternal chill of its watery world, there is no place it can take refuge. It cannot curl up like a wolf or a bear. There are no warm caves in which it can hide. It cannot bask in the sun like a turtle on a rock. All its warmth must come from inside it. To produce enough heat, whales have a high metabolism. All living things create energy and warmth within themselves. This is a chemical process that is called metabolism. The whale's metabolism works at a very high rate, like an internal furnace operating at top draft. This gives the whale the needed heat to keep warm in spite of the amount that is taken from it by the water. It also gives whales the energy to move ceaselessly. In cold water whales do not sleep, and even in the warm tropics they only nap for short periods. Whales cannot sleep deeply like humans. They can only doze, waken to take a breath, and then doze again.

There is still another way the whale keeps warm. Its thick layer of blubber, just under the skin, holds in the heat of its body like an overcoat. There may be twenty tons of blubber on the largest whales. The Greenland whales, which spend their whole lives in the Arctic, have a layer of blubber two feet thick. This permanent insulation prevents loss of heat, but it also presents the whale with a problem. Inside its blubber the whale is like a man with only one suit. There are times when it is too hot. When the whale exerts itself with rapid swimming it might die of overheating if it did not have some way to cool off.

Dogs pant. Horses sweat. Whales can do neither, but their fins, which have no blubber, are used to get rid of excess heat. The fins have a rich blood supply. When the whale needs to cool off, an extra supply of warm blood is sent to the surface of the fins, where it will be cooled by the water streaming past.

Fortunately for the whale, the temperature of the sea does not go to such great extremes, or rise and fall as sharply, as the air to which land animals must adjust. Temperatures on land range from way below zero to something in the hundreds, and even in the same spot there may be a great change from day to night or from season to season. In the sea there is a difference of only forty or fifty degrees between the waters of the tropics, where the temperature is in the seventies, and the poles, where it is near freezing.

In all animals the outer covering, or hide, must be suited to the animal's surroundings. Elephants, for instance, are protected from the heat and the thorny shrubbery of their homeland by a thick, leathery hide. The whale meets neither heat nor thorns and needs no such protection. Its great body is covered with a skin that is designed to help it move swiftly through the water. It is very thin and as smooth as glass. The hides of land animals have glands to oil their hair and sweat glands to cool their bodies. Whales do not need these glands and they have disappeared. The skin of a whale is very sensitive. A stranded whale shudders when it is touched, and is very easily sunburned. Small captive whales such as dolphins like to be stroked and to scratch themselves. Their keepers often fasten a brush, with bristles up, on the bottom of the pool. The dolphins like to rub against it.

Almost every animal is prey to parasites, and the whale is no exception. There is a small, snakelike fish that lives by attaching its mouth to a larger creature and hanging on as it sucks nourishment from the body of the host. This creature, called a lamprey, attaches itself to a whale. When it finally drops off, its mouth leaves a round white scar on the whale's dark hide. There are also small crablike creatures that burrow into the skin of some whales. On others, barnacles attach themselves. A large whale has been found carrying a thousand pounds of barnacles. No one knows if these parasites cause whales to itch, but if they do there is no easy way for the whale to scratch. Perhaps, if the water is not too deep, they rub itching parts on rocks. It has been

24

suggested that one reason whales leap out of the water and fall flat on the surface may be to quiet their itching hides.

The skeleton of the whale differs from that of land animals in that it is not designed to bear weight, but to anchor giant muscles. There are forty tons of muscle in a hundred-ton whale. There is a great mass of muscle in the lower back to move the tail, which drives the whale through the water. The bones of a whale are light and spongy, and contain a great deal of oil which whalers extract by boiling.

The great whales have immense jawbones. In some species they are curved like the tusks of elephants. In the old days whalers liked to bring home these bones as souvenirs. They often made arched gateways, some big enough for a horse and carriage to pass through.

The skeletons of all mammals have many things in common no matter how different their shape. For instance, both mice and giraffes have seven bones in the neck. So do whales. But the neck bones of whales are pressed close together and bend very little. They cannot turn their heads, but must always look straight ahead. On the other hand, the backbone is quite supple. The whale can bend its great body in an astonishing way.

The most flexible part of the whale is the tail, which moves it through the water. The tails of fish are vertical, that is up and down, like the rudder of a boat, and they swim by swishing their tails from side to side. The tail of the whale ends in huge paddles called flukes, that are horizontal to the surface. To swim, a whale beats its flukes against the water, like a frogman swimming with his feet tied together. Some whales have a small dorsal fin to help

25

them balance, but some get along without one. Whales do not use their flippers for swimming, but for balance and to help steer.

When a man swims he must raise his face out of the water to breathe. Whales have solved the problem of breathing by having their nostrils on top of their heads. Their blowholes have elastic sides that close tightly while the whale is under water. When the whale comes to the surface the muscles relax while the whale lets out a breath and takes another lungful of air.

Normally, baleen whales do not dive very deep. Most of their food floats in the top thirty feet of water and there is no reason to go below it. However, we know that they can go down into the depths if they choose to. A harpoon carrying a pressure gauge has been attached to a large baleen whale called a fin whale. It showed that the whale dove down to a depth of 1,164 feet.

Baleen whales usually stay under for ten to fifteen minutes, and then rise to breathe. Naturally, a whale's breathing becomes faster the more it exerts itself. A whale that is being chased swims at top speed and pants like a running horse. It must surface more often to breathe. By chasing whales in fast boats, whalers are able to force them to the surface to be shot.

Land mammals cannot breathe and swallow at the same time. Whales can. The nasal passages of land animals have specialized cells that filter out dust and moisten air. Because sea air is clean and moist, whales do not need these special cells and they have disappeared.

Whales have a larynx, or voice box, in the same place as other mammals, but they have no vocal cords. One of the mysteries of the great whales is how they make their extraordinary sounds.

26

When a whale comes to the surface and lets out its breath there is what looks like a fountain of spray, called a spout. Each kind of whale makes a spout of a particular shape, and this is one way that whalers can tell them apart. The blue whale, the largest of all whales, shoots up a plume twenty feet high. Another species of whale, called the right whale, blows two spouts to form a V. The spout of the whale makes it appear that the whale has breathed in water, but this is not the case. The spout can be seen for the same reason a person's breath can on a cold day. The warm air in the lungs holds water vapor under pressure. When it escapes it becomes cool. The vapor turns to droplets of water that look like spray.

The lungs of the blue whale weigh as much as a ton, but compared to the size of the whale's body they are rather small. The whale makes up for this, to some extent, by taking deep breaths. It empties and refills its lungs completely each time it breathes.

While it swims under water the whale, of course, holds its breath, but its body continues to use oxygen. A man can hold his breath for only a minute or two, but whales regularly go without a breath for five, or ten, or twenty minutes. The sperm whale can stay below the surface for an hour or more. To make it possible for them to go so long without breathing, whales have a special ability to store oxygen in the blood and in the muscles. The circulation of their blood is also regulated in a special way, so that during a long dive less oxygen is sent to parts of the body that can get along with less. Instead, oxygen is sent directly to the heart and the brain, which cannot do without it even for a short time.

Atlantic Bottlenose Dolphin

Chapter Four
Senses of Whales

(diagram showing echolocation)

Chapter Four
Senses of Whales

Land mammals depend on their five senses—sight, hearing, smell, touch, and taste—to inform themselves of their surroundings. In most cases the senses of sight and smell are the most useful and highly developed. The senses of whales, living in a world of water, have developed differently. Hearing is the sense on which they rely the most. The sea is full of sound. The tiny vibrations that make up a sound travel four and a half times as fast through water as they do through air. They also lose less energy as they move, and a sound may travel a long way before it dies out. In one experiment the sound of an explosion in the water off Australia was picked up several hours later by a listening device near Bermuda. It had traveled at a rate of one mile per second.

Whalers have long known that whales have very acute hearing. In hunting whales they found their quarry could be frightened by the tiniest sound. In the Arctic, Eskimos who hunt whales in small boats sit quietly, slipping their paddles into the water with care to avoid even a splash. Whales have been reported to react when another whale was harpooned twenty miles away.

The opening of the whale's ear is so small it can hardly be seen. On land, external ears act like a funnel and help an animal collect the sound waves that pass through the air. But in the sea big ears would be a hindrance, and whales have given them up. The muscles that used to move them are still there, under the skin, showing that they once existed. All that can now be seen of the whale's ear is a tiny hole on each side of the head behind the eye.

A man under water can hear sound, but because his skull bones conduct vibrations, it seems to come from everywhere at once. Whales avoid this by means of special skull cavities that block confusing vibrations, and so they can tell very well from where a sound is coming. A mystery of the whale's ear is that the semicircular canals, which provide balance, are remarkably small. They are no larger in a dolphin than in a hamster.

In the ocean, eyes have a limited use. Below the surface of the water it becomes increasingly dark the deeper one goes. Only ten per cent of the light striking the surface goes down as far as thirty feet. Below that depth a big whale could hardly see its flipper before its face. At a thousand feet below the surface there is only the dimmest twilight, and below seventeen hundred feet there is darkness. Furthermore, it is light only during the hours of sunlight, but whales are active day and night.

The eyes of whales are able to make the most of dim light. At the back of the eye there is a surface, called a *tapetum lucidum,* that reflects light. Cats and other animals of the night have the same thing. It is this that makes an animal's eyes shine in the dark when they are struck by a beam of light. The whale also has more of the cells that respond to light—called rods—than do most mammals.

Whales do not need eyebrows or eyelashes to protect their eyes from dust and sweat, but they do have eyelids for protection. Instead of tears, they produce a film of oil that covers their eyeballs and protects them from saltwater. The eye itself is quite small for such a big animal. In a big whale the eyes are about twice the size of the eyes of a cow. The color is brown, and they are placed just behind the corners of the mouth. There have been no tests to show how well baleen whales can see, either through air or under the sea, but we know that dolphins can see very well when their heads are out of water.

On land the sense of smell plays a big part in the lives of most mammals. Fish also can smell under water. But if whales inhaled water they would drown, and so they have to get along without this sense. Their smelling apparatus has all but disappeared. Possibly some kinds of whales can detect smells when their blowholes are out of water, but ordinarily there is not much above the surface to smell. It is safe to say that the sense of smell does not play much of a part in their lives. However, their tongues have taste buds and quite probably they taste their food and chemicals dissolved in the water they take into their mouths.

The brain of the whale is very large. In fact the brain of the sperm whale is the largest of any creature on earth. It weighs about seventeen pounds. Though the blue whale is larger than the sperm, its brain is not quite as large. It weighs about fifteen pounds. Next to the whale, the elephant has the largest brain. It averages eleven pounds. A human brain weighs three pounds.

Since nature seldom provides animals with useless organs, scientists have spent a good deal of time wondering how the whale uses this great mass of brain tissue. Intelligence of the sort that human beings possess does not necessarily increase as the brain increases in size, but large brains can be used for things other than humanlike thought. Most scientists believe that whales—the toothed whales especially—are highly intelligent animals. Dolphins have been shown to have good memories, the ability to solve many problems, and to communicate with each other to quite an extent. However, it is not likely that the big brains of whales indicate that they think the way humans do, or that they have any sort of "super" intelligence. Probably a great deal of their brain is concerned with their highly developed sense of hearing. They may use this sense in ways that are still mysterious to us.

Whales are social animals. Their relationship with other whales plays a great part in their lives. The small whales such as dolphins stay close to each other and move in tight-knit groups. We know enough about their lives to know that they have strong feelings about each other. They respond to each other in many ways that are familiar to human beings. They play, they fight, court each other, mate, and care for and train the young. They even come to the aid of a wounded comrade, lifting it with their heads and holding it with its blowhole up out of the water when it is in danger of sinking and drowning.

Baleen whales swim together, too, but in smaller groups and spread farther apart. This is probably because they must eat such huge amounts that if they crowded together there would not be enough food to go around. It is possible that they keep in touch even over great distances, sending and receiving signals that tell members of the group where their comrades are and what they are doing. Pairs of baleen whales—male and female—often travel together. Possibly, mated pairs in some species stick to each other for life. Baleen whales, too, will often try to help each other in moments of distress. Females fight fiercely to defend their young.

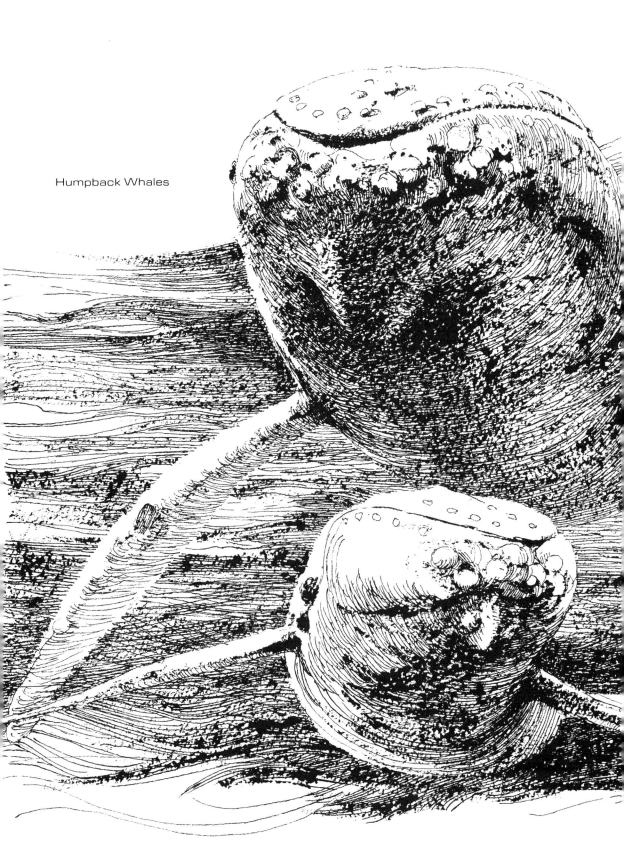

Humpback Whales

Chapter Five
Life Cycle of Whales

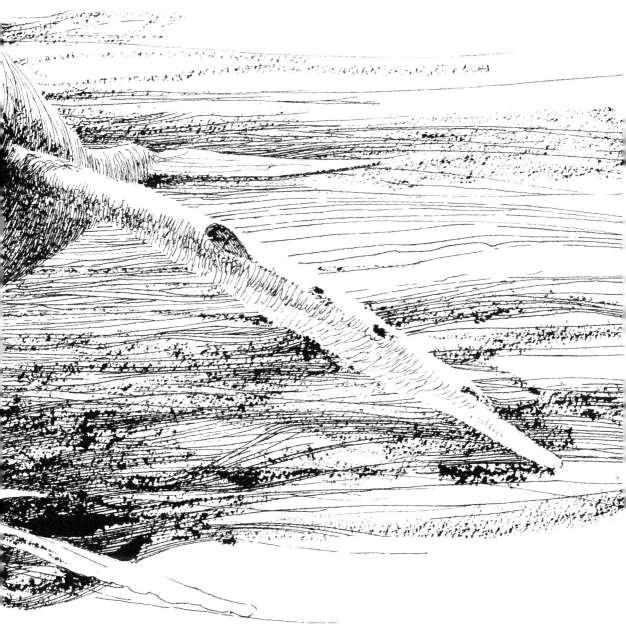

Chapter Five
Life Cycle of Whales

The most vital thing in the lives of whales is, of course, their food. The toothed whales are hunters. They pursue schools of fish and snatch their prey with their sharp teeth. Some species, such as the sperm whale, dive deep in search of boneless, tentacled creatures called squid. The baleen whales feed slowly, more like cows in a pasture. Because plankton is so abundant it is an ideal food supply for large animals. The other very large sea creatures, such as the forty-foot basking shark, the fifty-foot whale shark, and the huge manta ray, also feed on plankton.

As it does on land, all life in the sea begins with plants. Plants may be very tiny. Some consist of only a few cells and are so small they cannot be seen by the naked eye. Floating by the millions in the sea, such plants are food for tiny animals not much larger than themselves. When both are so tiny, we distinguish between plants and animals mainly according to how they nourish themselves. Only plants can create living tissue from lifeless elements. Plants are able to combine carbon dioxide and water by means of sunlight to nourish themselves and grow. Animals can live only on other living things, or things that once were alive.

On land we think of the warm tropics as producing the greatest growth of plants. In the sea things are different. There are more tiny sea plants in the cold waters near the North and South Poles than in the warmer seas near the equator. This is partly because cold water holds more oxygen and carbon dioxide than warm water does. It is also because the surface water near the poles contains a great deal of plant food made up of the dead bodies of plants and animals and other waste products. On land we call this material fertilizer.

In the sea such stuff normally sinks to the bottom, where it cannot be used by living plants which must stay near the top in the sunlight. But near the poles there are places where cold water from the ice caps meets warm water from the tropic seas. This results in an "upwelling," a strong current rising from the bottom. The upwelling water carries up sunken debris the way rising smoke carries up sparks. It provides an endless supply of fertilizer for the tiny plants floating in the sunlit surface water. For this reason the cold, gray, polar seas that look so wintry and dead are really bubbling springs of life. They produce many times more living material than do the transparent blue waters of the tropical oceans.

In the summer season there is also more sunshine at the poles than there is nearer the equator. This, of course, is because during the year the earth tilts in such a way that first one pole and then the other is facing the sun. In the polar winter the sun shines for only a brief time each day. In the summer it shines almost continually. Plants thrive in the long hours of sunlight and grow much more rapidly than they do where night and day are more evenly divided.

The carpets of sea plants floating near the surface of the water are like meadows of grass on land. They provide pasturage for many different kinds of small animals. There are wormlike creatures, of all sizes and shapes. There are snails and jellyfish. In the Antarctic one of the most abundant little animals is a small shrimp whose scientific name is *Euphausia superba Dana*. It is also called krill. In the Antarctic it is the main food of baleen whales.

In certain parts of the sea, krill swarm in such fantastic numbers that their reddish bodies form a rusty raft thirty feet thick spread over several square miles of ocean. The individual animal is a creature of great beauty. It is about two and a half inches long. Like a lobster or a shrimp it has a shell, feelers, and many legs. It is mostly red, but there is a bright green area where the green plants in its stomach show through its body. Its black eyes are held forward like headlamps. Its feathery legs paddle it forward, but it can shoot backward with a stroke of its tail if its antennae give it warning of danger. This may enable it to escape from a small enemy, but it is no defense against a whale. Baleen whales simply swim through swarms of krill with their mouths open, engulfing them by the millions. The stomach of a big whale may hold a ton of krill.

Baleen whales roam the entire ocean, but their comings and goings are not aimless. They swim from the equator to the poles and back to the equator on a regular schedule. This schedule is marvelously arranged so that they are in the right place at the right time to fulfill their different needs.

When spring comes to the polar regions the whales arrive to feed on the new crop of krill and other plankton. As the days lengthen the plants grow and the krill hatch from eggs and form their dense swarms. The whales graze through the long polar days. They are storing up fat, like money in the bank, saving it for the winter days when there will be no food.

Summer at the poles is the time when mother whales wean their young. For over a year the mothers have fed them with rich milk. In the Antarctic or Arctic, surrounded by plenty of food, the young learn to feed themselves like adults.

The adult female whales that have no young with them have mated the previous winter. They carry unborn young. The enormous supply of food makes it possible for the unborn whale to grow in the womb at a fantastic rate.

After three months or so of almost constant daylight, autumn darkness begins to fall on the Antarctic. The pastures of plankton wither. Then the whales start to move back to the warm waters of the equatorial seas. It is a journey of thousands of miles.

They find very little to eat on the way, but they have stored up so much fat that they are still strong when they reach the tropics. They will need this strength, for there will be little food during the winter.

Summer is the time for feeding. Winter is the time for mating and for birth. The females that have weaned their calves, as the young of whales are called, are now free of their responsibility. In the warm water of their winter home they mate again and begin to nourish a new life. The period of time from mating to birth, called the gestation period, is about a year. By mating in winter, the whales have ensured that their young will also be born in winter and that the newborn whale will find itself in warm waters as it begins its life.

No one has yet seen the birth of a baleen whale. Land animals are born headfirst, but great whales are probably born tail first. This avoids the chance of the baby whale breathing water while it is being born. Scientists have watched the birth of dolphins in tanks, and they do emerge tail first. As soon as they are born they rise to the surface for a breath of air. Most land animals are quite helpless when they are first born, but newborn whales swim with ease. Within a few minutes after birth little dolphins are swimming beside their mothers, diving and rising to breathe just as the mothers do. Baleen whales must do the same.

Nursing under water also presents special problems. If the milk glands and nipples of the female stuck out as they do in land animals, they would interfere with swimming and be liable to injury. In a female whale the glands and nipples are hidden within slits in the lower part of the belly, but she can push the

40

nipple out so that the calf can grab it in its mouth. The whale calf has no soft lips to hold the nipple tight, so it cannot suck the way a colt or a puppy can. Instead, it grasps the nipple between its tongue and the roof of its mouth. The mother has muscles which squirt the milk down the infant's throat.

Whale milk is creamy white. It tastes slightly fishy and it is very rich—three or four times as concentrated as cow's milk. Scientists guess that a big whale gives more than a hundred and thirty gallons of milk a day.

Infant whales are huge babies. They must be to survive. Land animals such as dogs and bears are born in a nest and are warmed by the bodies of their mother and brothers and sisters. Whales must warm themselves from the instant they leave their mother's body. To do this they must be large. A newborn blue whale weighs two tons and is twenty-five feet long—almost a third the length of its mother. Every day while it is nursing it grows two inches and gains a hundred pounds.

After it is weaned, the young whale must spend several years growing up. No one is quite sure how long this period lasts in different species. Scientists guess that the largest whales are old enough to mate at six. By then they have completed eighty-five per cent of their growth.

How long whales can live until they die a natural death is also unknown. In most mammals, childhood takes up a sixth to an eighth of the total life span. If the childhood of a blue whale lasts six years we might then reckon that it could live six or eight times as long, or between thirty-six and forty-eight years. An old harpoon found in a whale when it was killed has been identified after forty years. Another was found after thirty-two years; but naturally we do not know how much longer the whales might have lived, nor how old they were when first harpooned.

The scientists who study whales would give a great deal to be able to tell the ages of the whales that are killed by the whaling industry. Unfortunately, the only clue to the age of a grown baleen whale is found in a waxy earplug that appears to add layers throughout the whale's lifetime. But how often a layer is added—whether every six, twelve, or eighteen months, or every two years—has not been proven.

A matter of dispute among scientists is how many whales of each kind still remain. There is no accurate way to count them. Records are kept of the number of each kind that are killed by the whalers. As the number grows less, scientists guess that fewer are killed because there are fewer in the sea.

It is obvious that if more whales are killed than are born, there eventually will be no whales. The number born, of course, depends on the number of females to bear them. From year to year scientists have made various guesses about the total numbers of various species that still exist. These are only guesses and cannot be proven true. Many scientists have warned that the number of whales is shrinking at a dangerous rate. The Russians and the Japanese, who hunt whales and kill thousands every year, argue that there are still plenty left in the sea.

As in so many cases where man deals with nature, we are going ahead and doing something—killing whales—without being sure what the result will be. It would be of great value if biologists could find a way to discover the true numbers and birthrates of whales. In the meantime only one thing is sure: If we kill off too many whales, so that a species becomes extinct, we can never bring it back.

Chapter Six
The Rorquals

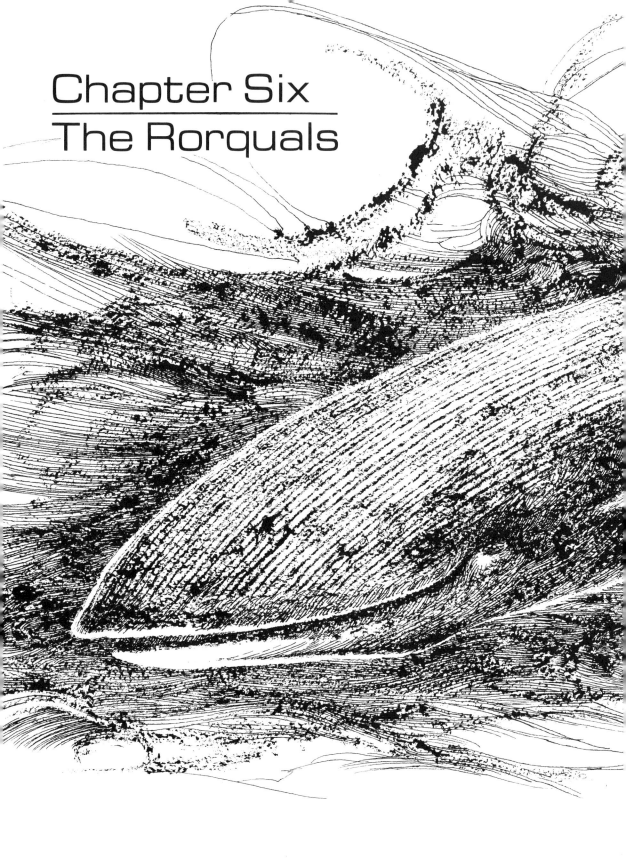

Blue Whale

Chapter Six
The Rorquals

The baleen whales are divided by scientists into ten species. Six of the ten species are closely related. They are called "rorquals," a name given them by the Norwegians who were the first to hunt them. It means "tubed whale." The tubes are a series of deep pleats or grooves that run along the whale's underside from chin to midsection. It is likely that the pleats allow its throat to expand as it takes in water with its food.

The rorquals are graceful, streamlined whales. They all have a small, crescent dorsal fin and a powerful tail that drives them through the water at high speed. Some can go as fast as thirty miles an hour.

The heads of rorquals are long and tapered. The lower jaw is undershot: The rim of the upper jaw fits into the lower the way a lid fits into a teapot. A small brown eye is set near each corner of the enormous mouth. There is an upward groove around the corners of the mouth that makes it look as though the whale is smiling.

The biggest rorqual is the gigantic blue whale. Next is the fin whale, which is middle-sized. There are three small rorquals —the sei, Bryde's whale, and the Minke. These five species look much alike. The sixth rorqual is the humpback whale. It is less tapered and doesn't look much like the others, but it has the pleats and so is considered a member of the group.

The rorquals swim in oceans all over the world. They feed in the rich waters of the North and South Poles and migrate to warmer waters to give birth and mate. In the tropical and sub-tropical oceans they spread out over vast stretches of water and are not easy to find, but when they are at the poles they are concentrated in a much smaller area. It is here that the whalers hunt them down.

In the early days of whaling the rorquals were not hunted, because they were too fast for sailors rowing whaleboats. Also, when they die their bodies sink. Modern machines have overcome both of these problems. There are now fast boats that can run down the speediest whale. A way to keep dead whales afloat so that they can be hauled aboard has also been found. After a rorqual has been killed, the whalers fill its body with compressed air which makes it float.

The lion is sometimes called King of Beasts. An ancient people, the Phoenicians, called the whale Lord of the Fish. Surely this is a good description of the largest rorqual, the blue whale. It is so big that it is hard to imagine as a living creature. The biggest blue whales are over a hundred feet long. One of them would be longer than a railroad car, and twenty feet high at the mid-section. This is about as high as a two-story house. The blue whale is by far the largest creature living today. It may be the largest creature that has ever lived. It is far bigger than even the greatest of the dinosaurs.

A big blue whale weighs well over a hundred tons. Blue whales gain and lose gigantic amounts of weight according to the season. In their polar summer they eat constantly and may gain thirty or forty tons. This fat is then used up during the winter, when they get little to eat. Although no one has proved it, it is thought possible that a really large, fat blue whale could weigh two hundred tons. This is more than the weight of a ship the size of the Mayflower including her passengers.

The power stored within a big whale is equally extraordinary. Blue whales cruise along at six to eight miles per hour. If they are in a hurry they can steam along at more than twice this speed for several hours. If they are frightened they can surge forward at twenty miles an hour. There is a grisly record of a blue whale that was struck with a harpoon and made fast to a catcher boat. It pulled the boat, which was ninety feet long, in spite of its engines going full speed astern, for seven hours over fifty miles of ocean.

Blue whales are actually a mottled slate color. They are paler underneath. Sometimes their hides seem to turn bright yellow when a film of algae blooms on their skin. Algae are microscopic plants like those that make scum on the bottom of a pond. Because of this yellow color, blue whales were known in old whaling days as sulphur-bottom whales.

Blue whales like very deep water. They seldom approach shore, but now and then a blue whale is stranded. Whether this happens because the whale is sick or has lost its way no one can say.

48

Blue whales sometimes come together in groups of five or six, but they do not form large herds, at least as far as we are able to see. Possibly the members of the herd are so far apart that we do not realize they are traveling together.

Whalers often find a pair of blue whales, male and female, swimming together. If the female is shot the male will not leave her side; this enables the whalers to take him also. Females are not so loyal and will swim away from a wounded mate. Young blue whales are full of curiosity, and when a boat approaches them they often swim toward it to investigate.

Because blue whales are the largest, they are also the most valuable to whalers. Hundreds of thousands were killed over a a period of forty years. Finally, in 1964, there were so few left that the officials in charge of whaling, a group called the International Whaling Commission, decided to protect the remaining blue whales. There is now a ban on killing them. No one knows how many blue whales are left. Some scientists have even suggested that they may become extinct. They fear that there may be so few left that they will be unable to find mates in the vast, trackless seas. However, a few blue whales are sighted every year, so we know that there are still some on earth.

The next largest whale is the fin whale. Although it is smaller than the blue, it is still a tremendous creature. It may be seventy-five or eighty feet long—which is longer than most houses—and weigh fifty or sixty tons. It is the slimmest rorqual, with a pointed snout and tail and a sickle-shaped dorsal fin. Its back is a dark slate gray that may look black as it surges out of water, or greenish if it carries a film of algae. The dark color shades to creamy white on the underside. The fin whale's pleats make gray furrows from chin to midsection. An odd feature of the fin whale's color pattern is that the right side of the lower jaw is always very light and the left side very dark.

Like the blue whale, the fin can be found in all the oceans, but it does not go quite as far into the polar ice in summer, nor as close to the equator in winter. The fin whale eats fish as well as plankton and sometimes follows schools of fish close to shore. It often feeds swimming on its side with its mouth open, and then turns on its back so that its lower jaw is partly out of water as it swallows.

Fin whales can swim as fast as, or faster than, blues. They do not leap out of water—or breach, as it is called—unless they are wounded or excited; but then their entire length may shoot up like a rocket out of the depths.

Fin whales do not usually form large groups. More often, they swim in pairs, or sometimes three or four together. Now and then, however, whalers have found them gathered by the dozens. The fin whales were once the most plentiful of baleen whales. As the blue whales became scarcer the whalers turned to the fins, and they have killed them in large numbers. No one knows how many are left. Perhaps a good many thousands, but they are still being killed by Russian and Japanese whalers.

One step down the scale in size come two smaller rorquals: the sei and Bryde's whale. The sei is named by the Norwegians after a kind of fish that this whale follows off the coast of Norway. Bryde's whale is found in warmer waters around the world, but is more rare. These two rorquals are much alike and look like small fin whales. Bryde's whale grows to forty-five feet in length and the sei to sixty. The sei has baleen that ends in fringe as soft and fine as fleece. With this it can strain very small creatures out of the water. The sei whale also eats small fish. The Japanese call it the sardine whale. It twists and turns in the water as it pursues its prey. For short sprints the sei is the fastest whale. It has been timed at thirty miles per hour. Because seis are comparatively small they are less valuable to whalers than the blue and the fin. Until recently they have not been so heavily hunted. Many thousands are still found in the Antarctic each year.

The smallest rorqual is called the little piked whale, or Minke. It is only thirty feet long. It looks like a very small fin whale. It swims in icy seas near the poles and goes deeper into the Antarctic ice than any other whale. An explorer, Sir Ernest Henry Shackleton, named the Bay of Whales after finding a great number of Minke whales playing among the ice floes. Groups of a thousand Minkes have been seen. It is a very playful whale and often jumps right out of the water, or stands up in the water and looks about. Sometimes Minkes rest their heads on the floes. In the northern half of the world Minkes visit the coast of Europe, and have even swum up the Thames to London. Minkes have been heavily hunted by the Norwegians and the Japanese, but there are still large numbers of them.

The humpback whale is quite different from the other rorquals, but it is considered one because it has pleats. The other rorquals are long and slim, but the humpback is rounder and has a huge head. A small, rounded dorsal fin gives it a humpbacked appearance when its back comes out of the water. Humpbacks are huge beasts, fifty feet long.

The humpback is usually black on its back with various

patches of white on its undersides. It is a gaily piebald whale. No two are quite alike. The humpback has a series of knobs or bumps on its head and jaws and on the forward edge of its flippers. Each sprouts one or two coarse bristles. It is possible that they are sense organs of a kind we do not yet understand. Another odd feature of this whale is its long winglike flippers. They are as much as eighteen feet long. This is far longer than the flippers of any other whale.

The humpback is the most athletic and playful of the giant whales. It often leaps and falls flat on its side or back, smacking the water with a mighty splash. Sometimes it swims on its back or turns a whole somersault in the water.

Long ago a whaling man, Captain Charles Scammon, wrote a description of the love play of humpbacks: "In the mating season they are noted for their amorous antics. At such times their caresses are of the most amusing and novel character. . . . When lying by the side of each other . . . [they] frequently administer alternate blows with their long fins, which love-pats may, on a still day, be heard a distance of miles. They rub each other with these same huge and flexible arms, rolling occasionally from side to side, and indulging in other gambols which can easier be imagined than described."

This lively whale makes the most musical sounds that have been discovered in the sea. Scientists listening with special underwater microphones called hydrophones have found that humpbacks sing long, complicated songs. Their sounds can be called songs for the same reason that the sounds of birds can be called songs. They consist of a series of notes that is often repeated. Birds sing short, rapid songs that fit their small size. Humpbacks sing long, slow songs, with each note distinct. This also seems right for their size.

The voice of the humpback doesn't sound quite like anything on earth and yet it reminds the listener of many familiar sounds. Sometimes it sounds like an orchestra of musicians playing off key. Sometimes it sounds like a baby crying far away. The whale may follow this with groans, bleats, and moos; or with a noise like a rusty hinge squeaking or a motorcycle starting up. And sometimes the whales sing with high silvery voices, the way fairies of the deep would sing if there were fairies of the deep.

We do not know how humpbacks make these sounds or why they make them. The best guess is that through these songs the whales keep in touch with each other. They may exchange simple information—a message such as "I am here. Where are you?" Land animals leave a track or a scent that allows others of their kind to locate them. Whales cannot do this, but sounds traveling long distances under water could enable migrating whales to keep in touch with each other.

There were once great numbers of humpbacks in both the northern and southern seas. They migrate from the poles to the equator, and their route often takes them close to shore. Because they are slow swimmers they are easy to kill, and have been hunted for many years. Now only a few survivors of the species remain. One of the places where they can still be found near our shores is in the waters around the island of Bermuda. In the early spring the migrating humpbacks pause there to feed and play and sing their mysterious songs.

Chapter Seven
Other Baleen Whales

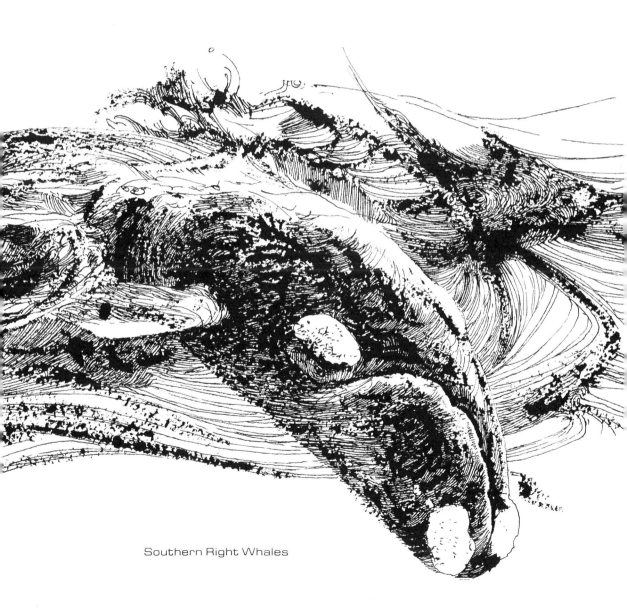

Southern Right Whales

Chapter Seven
Other Baleen Whales

The rarest of all the great whales is the one that was once the most plentiful. It is called the black right whale and it is now seldom seen. The black right whale, and its relative the Greenland right whale, were the first whales to be hunted so mercilessly that they became nearly extinct.

The black right whale is a huge, slow-swimming whale. It is easy to catch from an open boat. For this reason it was attacked by primitive hunters wherever it appeared along their shores. When it is dead its body floats, while that of a rorqual sinks. This gave it its name of right whale, meaning the "right" whale to catch.

Right whales are short and fat. A sixty-foot whale may be

forty feet around the middle. Its head is huge—one third the length of its body. Its jaws are curved and its mouth is like a cavern. The baleen hangs from the upper jaw like a fringed curtain. The right whale also has mysterious bumps on its chin and snout. There is a large, strange growth on top of its head called a "bonnet."

There were once thousands of black right whales in the warmer waters of both the Atlantic and Pacific. In our part of the world, whaling began in the eleventh century. At that time there were many black right whales off the coast of France. A people called the Basques, who live on the shores of the Bay of Biscay, were the first Europeans to kill whales on a large scale. Soon others joined in. The whales in European waters lasted some five hundred years, but by the sixteenth century there were no more on that side of the Atlantic.

As America was settled, whalers began to hunt off our shores and then to pursue the whales north into the colder waters. Eventually, scarcely any black right whales could be found in the entire Atlantic. In the Pacific, the black right whales were not killed in great numbers until about a hundred years ago. Then a great fleet of whaling ships of many nations swept over the Pacific. They polished off most of the black right whales within fifty years. There are no longer enough black right whales anywhere to make it worthwhile to hunt them. Yet, luckily, a few escaped the whalers and have carried on their kind. Now and then black right whales are glimpsed from ships in many parts of their former range.

In the southern oceans a smaller species of right whale is also sometimes seen. It is called the pygmy right whale and is only about twenty feet long. These whales are quite rare and little is known about them.

At about the time that the black right whale became scarce in waters close to Europe, whalers discovered its northern cousin, the Greenland right whale. This whale is very much like the black right whale except that its head is even more huge and its mouth more grotesquely curved. A whaling captain named William Scoresby who had the experience of looking into the open mouth of a Greenland whale wrote later that it looked as big as a room and could contain a small boat together with its crew. He estimated that it was eight feet wide, twelve feet high, and fifteen feet deep. It must have been a moment the Captain would remember the rest of his life.

The Greenland whale stays within the seas surrounding the North Pole, and does not migrate to warmer waters even to give birth. Its calf is born wearing an extra-heavy suit of blubber so that it can withstand the cold. As these huge whales swim amid the floating ice they are able to push great floes of ice apart to make a passage.

Often the Greenland whales swim under the ice, breaking through it with their backs in order to breathe. Sometimes they are trapped where the ice is too thick even for their great strength, and they die. When Eskimos find the frozen body of a whale that has died in this way it is the occasion for a great feast.

British and Dutch whalers began to hunt Greenland whales in the early 1600's. The profits were huge. A single whale yielded twenty-five tons of oil, enough to pay for the trip. Other Europeans joined in the hunt. Hundreds of ships carrying thousands of men sailed for the polar seas. In the eighteenth century the Americans also began Arctic whaling. They moved into the north Pacific where they killed both black right and Greenland whales. By the end of the 1800's the Greenland whales were almost gone and most countries gave up the hunt. The British, however, went on. They followed the last whales into the deepest ice. They killed all sizes. At last, a whaling expedition was unable to find a single whale. Unknown to them, however, a handful had escaped into the vastness of the Arctic waters. Now and then a Greenland whale is seen in Hudson Bay or the Bering Sea. Sometimes Eskimos or Siberian natives capture one and rejoice at their good luck.

The baleen whale that can be seen most easily is the gray whale. Gray whales spend their summers feeding in the Bering Sea. In the autumn they migrate south to winter quarters off the coast of Baja California. In making this journey they pass quite close to the California shore. They can be seen from small boats or even from shore.

The gray whale is a cigar-shaped whale about fifty feet long. It has a slim and flexible body and a small head. It still has quite a few hairs on its head and lower jaw. There are three or four pleats on the throat, and so it seems to be halfway between the right whales, which have no pleats, and the rorquals, which have a great many.

Gray whales are found only in the Pacific Ocean. There were once a great many near the Japanese coast, but they have almost all been killed. Those that swim off California were also nearly wiped out by American whalers. None were seen for many years, but the few that were left managed to breed and increase. For the last thirty years or so they have been protected by law. Thanks to this, thousands of gray whales still swim along the California coast.

The migration of the gray whales is perhaps the longest journey made by any mammal. Only the humpback may travel as far. The distance from the summer pasture of the gray whales in the northern sea to their winter home is between four and six thousand miles, depending on the route they choose. To cover this distance the gray whales swim steadily for three months. They do not stop to eat, and probably rest very little.

No one knows how the whales find their way, but scientists believe that they use the position of the sun and stars as a guide and may also follow underwater landmarks. It is possible that the whales remember the distinct taste of the water that flows out of lagoons and estuaries along their route.

As the whales swim south they are on a tight schedule. Half the females are pregnant, and they must reach a safe place before they give birth. Babies born in the cold, rough waters of the open sea might die. Their destination is a number of lagoons scattered along the coast of Baja California. These lagoons are like great lakes of salt water connected to the sea by narrow channels. For the most part they are quite shallow. Their waters are warm and calm. They are ideal nurseries.

In these lagoons the females that have weaned their calves mate again. Here it is possible to witness the mating of great whales. They lie side by side in the water and there is a tremendous splashing and flurrying of the water with flippers and flukes as they press their giant bodies together.

Here, too, newborn calves can be seen swimming by their mothers' sides, rising and diving in perfect "step" with them wherever they go. The mothers spend the winter months lazing about the lagoon while the calves fatten and grow, preparing for the long journey north in the spring. The whales are perfectly gentle as long as they are not molested, but they are very protective of their young. In the old days when whalers came into the lagoons to hunt them the mother whales would fight fiercely. They smashed many a whaleboat with their flukes as they tried to save their calves.

Not long ago the managers of a large aquarium called Sea World, near San Diego, captured a baby gray whale alive. They transported it carefully by boat. When it arrived at Sea World, the calf, a female, was eighteen feet long. She weighed 4,300 pounds. She was named Gigi and put in a large tank where she soon settled down quite happily. Her keepers put together a feeding formula made of heavy cream, ground-up fish, cod-liver oil, and vitamins. In order to feed her the water in the pool was lowered so that she rested on the bottom. Then her trainer put a tube down her throat and poured in the formula. Gigi gained weight at the rate of twenty-seven pounds a day and grew a third of an inch a day.

To keep Gigi from being lonely, dolphins were put in the tank, and a young woman employed at Sea World made friends with her and often swam beside her. Gigi became extremely attached to her two human friends, the woman and the trainer. It was possible for either one of them to ride on her back. They taught her signals—light taps on the top of the head—telling her to stop or swim, and she obeyed them. Sometimes Gigi made strange, low-pitched sounds that seemed to come from deep inside her. Her trainer thought she was trying to talk to him.

At the end of a year at Sea World, Gigi had grown to nearly seven tons and was twenty-seven feet long. Scientists had made many interesting tests and observations. She was growing every day, and the time would soon come when she would be too big for the biggest pool at Sea World. It was decided to put her back in the sea before she got too big to be moved. In preparation for setting her free a radio transmitter was attached to her back. By this means it would be possible to trace her journey in the sea.

One morning Gigi was wrapped in a sling. A giant crane was brought to the side of the pool and the whale was hoisted out and put down on a foam rubber mattress on the bed of a huge truck. Wet blankets were draped over her to keep her skin comfortably wet. Her trainer stood beside her, patting her and soothing her as the truck drove down to the waterfront. She was lifted again and placed on a barge. The barge was towed four and a half miles out to sea. Then a crane lowered the sling holding Gigi into the water. She was once more free.

For some weeks scientists kept track of the signals coming from the transmitter on Gigi's back. Other gray whales were swimming north, and she swam with them. When she had swum about five hundred miles the scientists decided to follow her no farther. She has not been seen since, but there are many people who hope that she made the long journey safely. And there are many who find it a hopeful sign that at last a great whale has been in the power of human beings and been unharmed.

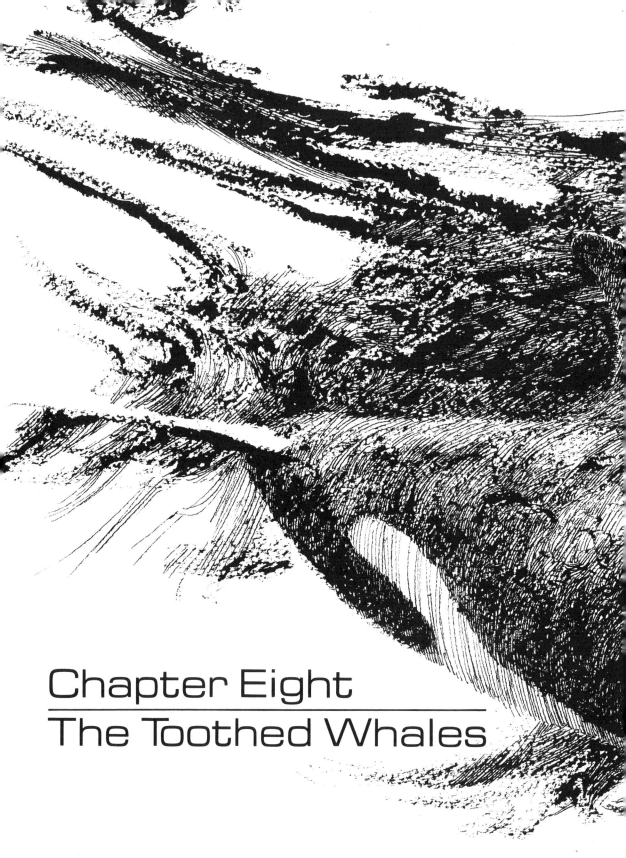

Chapter Eight
The Toothed Whales

Killer Whale

Chapter Eight
The Toothed Whales

The toothed whales are quite different from their cousins the baleen whales. Some, like the dolphins, feed near the surface and pursue fast-moving fish. In order to catch them their jaws have become long and narrow, almost like the beaks of birds. Other toothed whales feed in the depths, where they grasp the boneless bodies of squid. Their heads are blunt and they seem to have no features to make up a face. There is only the slit of the mouth and two tiny eyes.

The best-known toothed whales are those in the dolphin family. It is a large family. There are more than sixty species. The smallest species of dolphin is about five feet long. The largest dolphins are the thirty-foot killer whales.

We know a great deal about one particular kind of dolphin because many of them have been kept in captivity and biologists have been able to study them at close range. This is the Atlantic bottlenose dolphin. This species is often trained, and is familiar to many people who have seen Flipper and other dolphins perform on TV; bottlenoses are very often used in marine shows.

Atlantic bottlenose dolphins are found along our eastern shore south of Cape Cod. Dolphins of very similar species swim along the shores of the Pacific and Indian oceans. Bottlenose dolphins are gray, with dark and light shadings. They grow to be about ten feet long and to weigh as much as eight hundred pounds.

Bottlenose dolphins have beaklike snouts and sharp teeth. When they catch a fish they swallow it headfirst and whole. In captivity they eat about fifteen pounds of fish a day. It has also been discovered that they drink small amounts of seawater. At top speed they can swim eighteen miles per hour, but they usually cruise more slowly. When they are swimming at the surface they breathe once or twice a minute, but they can dive and hold their breath for seven minutes.

Dolphins live together in groups. Small groups of one or two females and their young, or mixed groups, join together to form large schools dominated by the largest males. Such a school may number a dozen dolphins or as many as a hundred. They go everywhere together. Sometimes they swim in ranks like soldiers.

There is constant cooperation among members of a school of dolphins. They feed together, cruise together, and rest together.

They have been seen working together to drive fish into a tight school were they could be more easily caught. If a school of dolphins is surrounded by a net, scouts will go out to try and find an exit or a way to break through the net. If they succeed the whole school follows. If there is something unusual in their path, scouts are sent to investigate and report back before the school goes on.

Dolphins are playful. They love to ride in the breaking wave that runs along at the bow of a ship. Sometimes they ride the surf near a beach just as human surfers do. At other times they leap and splash or toss some floating toy, such as a plank or buoy, or even a feather from a sea gull. They rub and touch each other a great deal. From an early age they show a great deal of sexual interest in each other.

Scientists have watched the birth of a dolphin to a mother in a tank. The young one is about three and a half feet long and weighs thirty pounds. It is born tail first and quickly goes to the surface for air. If it has any trouble the mother helps it up. The calf swims close to its mother. Her swimming creates an envelope of moving water that carries it along.

The calf nurses for a year or so on rich milk. Mothers take good care of their young. They also punish them for disobedience such as wandering too far or not coming when called. Punishment may be a nip or a slap with a flipper or flukes. Sometimes another female acts as an "aunt" and helps take care of the young one.

Adult dolphins are kind to the very young, but as the young grow older they are taught to respect the rules of dolphin life.

68

These are complicated, and young dolphins have a lot to learn. When they are old enough to leave their mothers' sides they spend a great deal of time romping. They chase and wrestle. One may tease another by dangling a toy in front of it and then racing off when the other reaches for it. In captivity they love to play ball with their trainers.

Dolphins are aware of each other as individuals. A trained dolphin has shown that it could recognize the whistling sounds of a number of different dolphins just as we recognize different people by their voices. Biologists believe there can be affection between adult dolphins as well as between mothers and young. Dolphins often try to protect each other or help each other in moments of trouble. A pair of dolphins will lift a sick comrade by putting their heads under its flippers.

The hearing of dolphins is wonderfully acute. Only bats have sharper ears. Since their ears are such tiny openings, some scientists think that they may also hear through their lower jaws. In any case, it has been proved that dolphins and other toothed whales have a strange and wonderful ability called echolocation. They send out a sound, or vibration, that bounces back from any object in its path and returns to be picked up by their keen ears. Tiny variations in the returning sound bring information about the size and shape of the object it has struck.

Dolphins can do astonishing things by echolocation, such as finding a nickel on the bottom of a pool or telling one kind of metal from another. The echolocating sound of dolphins is a series of clicks. They can make a whistling sound at the same time, and this is probably how they communicate with each other. They also make all sorts of strange squawks and squeals. They are very talkative beasts.

The killer whale doesn't look like a dolphin. It is bigger and has a blunt head. But it belongs to their family nonetheless. It is one of the handsomest beasts in the sea. It is flashily marked in black and white, sometimes tinged yellow, in a pattern something like the dress suit of penguins. Killers weigh as much as eight tons. They can move with flashing speed and power. They roam all the oceans in packs, hunting fish, birds, seals, and even great baleen whales.

Killers attack like wolves, surrounding their prey and snatching bites from it. Quite often they attack gray whales. They have the grisly habit of shoving with their snouts until the whale's mouth opens and they are able to bite off pieces of its tongue. Since there is no hiding place in the ocean and killers can easily outswim them, gray whales try to escape by lying perfectly still. This indicates that killers depend on disturbance in the water to locate their prey.

Although killers are so fierce in the wild, they are gentle in captivity. So are other predators such as lions and wolves. The secret seems to be a full stomach. If they are well fed and well treated, killer whales, or lions, have no motive for an attack on a human being. Killers can be trained like other dolphins. They are exhibited at a number of marine parks.

The pilot whale is another large dolphin. It is found from the Arctic to the Antarctic. It is about twenty feet long and has a shiny black hide that looks like the surface of an inner tube. It has a domed forehead, and no beak. Its small, pointed teeth are

70

adapted to catching squid. Pilot whales form large schools. Sometimes hundreds gather together. They are hunted for their oil and meat. Pilot whales are very attached to each other and follow their leaders even into danger. Sometimes whole schools are stranded. Then the unfortunate whales make a great many sounds. They roar, bellow, whistle, and snort. They whimper with a sound like that of a child.

We think of all whales as living in the sea, but there is a stranger group of small dolphins that live in tropical rivers. In the river Ganges in India there is a little dolphin known as the susu. The river is so muddy that little can be seen under water. The susu has become almost blind. It feeds on the bottom, digging out small creatures with its pointed snout. In the Amazon River in South America there is a similar dolphin called the boutu.

The white whale, or beluga, is about the same size as a pilot whale, but it is in a different family. Like the white bear, it is a creature of the North Pole. Its tough white hide reduces loss of heat. It swims under the sea ice using breathing holes made by seals. Like pilot whales, belugas make a great many sounds. They have been heard grunting and making groaning sounds, whistles, chirps, and squeaks. A few belugas have been kept in captivity and become very tame. About a hundred years ago a beluga was kept in a Boston aquarium. It was harnessed to a floating cart and drew a young lady around the tank.

The narwhal is another polar whale, in the same family as the beluga. It is a showy animal, twenty feet long with a light gray hide that is dappled with dark spots. The strangest thing about it, though, is its long twisted tusk. The narwhal has no teeth in the lower jaw, and only one pair in the upper. In males the right tooth grows straight ahead as long as nine feet, like a spear sprouting from its mouth. Several hundred years ago such tusks were brought to Europe and were thought to be the horns of a mythical horselike animal called the unicorn.

No one knows if the narwhal's tusk is useful. Perhaps male narwhals fight with their tusks or use them to chip breathing holes in the ice. Narwhals, like other toothed whales, are very social animals and swim in schools. They also make weird sounds that have been described as whistles, roars, and gurgles.

The least-known whales are a family commonly called beaked whales. They have the good fortune to be inedible, and so they have not been hunted as much as other whales. Furthermore, they stay in deep water where they feed on squid and are not often seen. There are about eighteen species of beaked whales. They range in size from fifteen to forty feet. Some species have rounded foreheads that give them a birdlike profile. Others have heads that slope like wine bottles and are called bottle-nosed whales. Since they feed on squid their teeth have become few, but the insides of their mouths are lined with what looks like pink terry cloth. This roughness helps them hold on to slippery, thrashing squid.

Like their dolphin cousins, beaked whales are social and swim in schools. They are playful and curious. In fact bottle-nosed whales are so trusting that it is difficult to drive them away from a boat. Like the other toothed whales, beaked whales help a wounded comrade and refuse to leave it. If they are stranded they make strange sounds, like a child sobbing or a pig in distress.

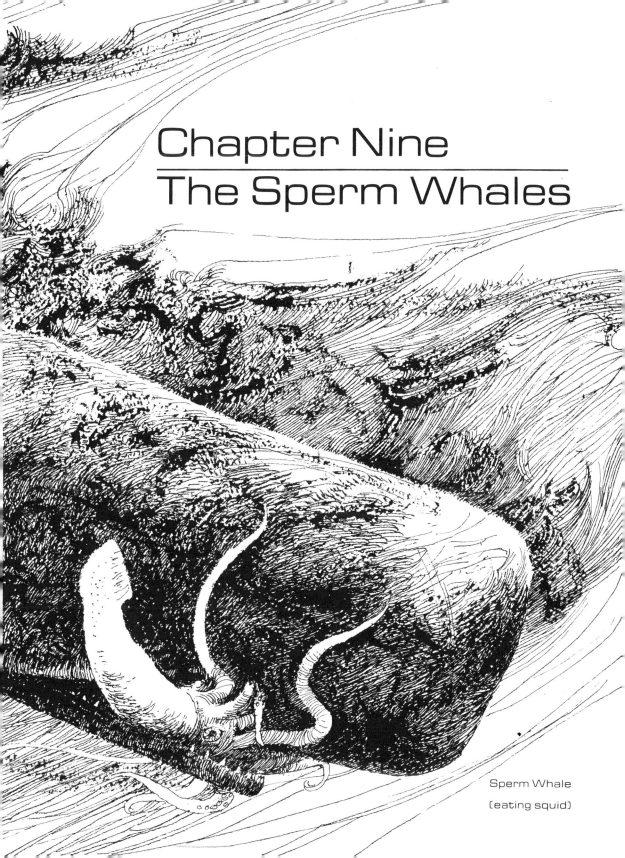

Chapter Nine
The Sperm Whales

Sperm Whale

(eating squid)

Chapter Nine
The Sperm Whales

The giant sperm whale has a family all to itself and its only close relative, the pygmy sperm, which is very like it except for size. The sperm whale is sixty feet long and has a peculiar shape. It has a monstrous head which is one third of its body length.

Its head is shaped like a huge box. The forehead is a cliff, eight or nine feet high. This is not the whale's skull, but a structure of tough tissue called the case that sits on top of the skull. Inside it is a ton or two of clear, oily liquid called spermaceti. This hardens to wax and makes very good candles. No one is quite sure why the sperm whale has this case of spermaceti, but biologists guess that it is concerned with sending and receiving sound signals.

The sperm's narrow mouth is on the underside of the case, which overhangs it. The lower jaw is a long, narrow blade, with massive round teeth that fit into sockets in the toothless upper jaw. Somehow the sperm clasps the bodies of writhing squid against the ridges in the roof of its mouth and sucks them down. The lower jaw is hinged so that it can gape open at a right angle to the head. An angry sperm whale with its mouth open is a fearsome sight.

The sperm dives deeper than any whale. For a deep dive the sperm raises its head, spouts a great plume, then curves its back and goes down steeply, with a farewell wave of its flukes. It stays below from fifteen minutes to an hour and a half. When it comes up it lets out air with an explosive spout that has a bad smell. After a long dive the whale must stay near the surface, spouting to ventilate its lungs. Old whalers used to say that a sixty-foot sperm whale weighed sixty tons, stayed down sixty minutes, and spouted sixty times.

Sperm whales roam all the oceans of the world, but the females are smaller than the males and never go into polar waters. They stay in the warm waters on each side of the equator.

Single males go far into the icy seas of the Arctic and Antarctic. They are found there along with the baleen whales.

Sperm whales do not form pairs to mate. Instead, a large male will have a harem of ten or fifteen wives. Sometimes he shares them with another old male. Males guard these wives and their children fiercely. Sometimes several harems join to form a larger school. As many as a hundred sperm whales have been seen together. It is the smaller males without wives that range into the far north and south.

Sperm whales stick to deep water because there they find the most squid. Squid are soft, boneless creatures with long arms, or tentacles. They are related to the snail and the octopus. They do not swim like fish, but are jet propelled, sending out streams of water that move them about with amazing speed. There are many species of squid. Those that sperm feed on are usually from three to six feet long. There is a legend that a monstrous squid, called the kraken, could rise from the deep and crush a ship in its clammy arms.

In fact squid fight for their lives. Their tentacles have sharp hooks that scar the heads of the sperm whales with a design of fine white lines. A squid's body also contains a horny beak that the sperm whale digests slowly. As many as twenty thousand beaks have been found in one whale's stomach. Sperm whales also swallow some fish, crabs, octopuses, and now and then a seal. Old shoes and net buoys have been found inside them, too.

Sometimes a lump of a stuff called ambergris is found in the intestines of a sperm whale, or even floating in the ocean. It is used in making perfume and is very valuable. It is formed around the sharp beaks of squid inside the whale's stomach in much the same way pearls are formed around grains of sand.

Sperm whales breed and give birth in warm waters. A female has a calf every two or three years. The newborn sperm whale is about fifteen feet long. It weighs about a ton. To nurse it, the mother turns on her side so that a teat is nearly out of water. Because the little sperm has such a peculiarly shaped mouth, it suckles in a peculiar way. It takes the teat in the corner of its mouth, for a few seconds only, and the milk is squirted down its throat.

In spite of their strangely shaped bulk, sperm whales are amazingly athletic. They can stand straight up with three quarters of their bodies above the water. They can also stand on their heads and wave their tails. Sometimes they breach three or four times in a row. When they do, the splashes can be heard for miles.

There are close ties between members of a group of sperm whales. They often leap, rise, and blow at the same time. Sometimes they swim side by side in rows or gather head to head, like a giant daisy, lashing the water with their flukes.

Sperm whales are easily frightened by sudden sounds. The steady hum of an engine doesn't alarm them, but the sound of an oar can put them to flight. Because of the way their eyes are placed, far back near the corners of the mouth, sperm cannot see directly in front of or behind themselves. Old whalers took advantage of this, coming up on them from the rear.

When alert to danger, a sperm may raise its head out of water and swim in a circle to look in all directions. Or it may hold its breath and lie perfectly still. Most often a frightened herd takes flight. When one member of a herd is frightened, it somehow sends warning signals to other whales, even at a distance of six or seven miles.

When an adult sperm is harpooned, the other whales may gather about it or they may stampede. Males come to the help of females, but do not help other males. Females flee when a male is hit by a harpoon, but they will not leave a wounded calf. A while ago Captain Jacques Cousteau, the French ocean explorer, reported that his ship accidentally hit a calf. The entire herd of twenty-seven whales gathered around the wounded creature.

In the old days of whaling, large male sperm whales, and even females, sometimes attacked open whaleboats in self-defense. When a sperm whale attacks, it turns on its side or back and charges with jaws gaping wide. Whale boats have been bitten in two. Angry whales clap their jaws together. The sound can be heard for miles. After smashing a boat, the whales would turn and bite the floating pieces. Sometimes, too, a furious whale might ram a boat or smash it with its flukes.

Large male sperm also fight each other for possession of a harem. Long ago whalers saw such a fight and have left a description. A large male sperm whale tried to join the harem belonging to another male. The two charged each other. They collided like locomotives. Then they seized each other's jaws and wrestled. Their thrashing made a boiling cauldron of spray. They bit great hunks of flesh from each other. They charged

80

and wrestled two or three times before the intruder gave up and fled. When the whalers harpooned the winner, they found he had a broken jaw.

Chapter Ten
To Save Whales

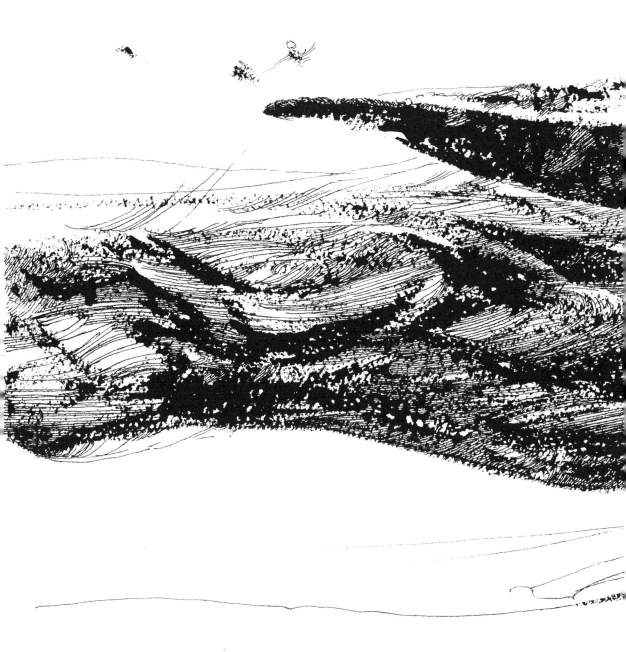

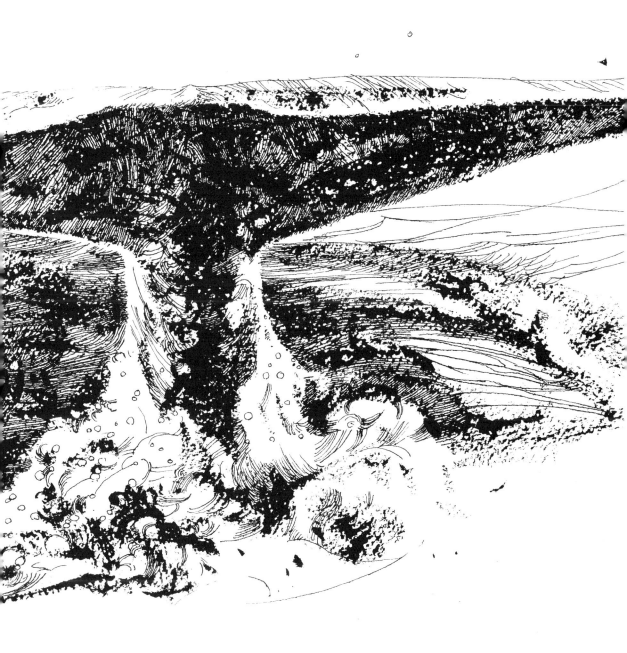

Chapter Ten
To Save Whales

In the past, the ships of many nations have joined the hunting of whales. The United States had a great whaling fleet of sailing ships. They roamed all the seas a hundred years ago and killed whales by the hundreds of thousands. But we have taken little part in modern whaling. ~stop here~

Modern whaling began about a hundred years ago, when Norwegian whalers began to use a kind of harpoon that was fired from a gun and exploded inside the whale. The Norwegians first used it to capture blue whales and fin whales in the North Atlantic. Quite soon these species were almost wiped out. The whalers then discovered that a gold mine of whales could be found near the South Pole when the whales went there to feed. From this time on, beginning in 1904, whaling fleets have gone to the Antarctic each season to kill whales. Now whales are becoming scarce even there, and the whalers are ranging over the whole Pacific ocean in their search for the last whales.

To the men who kill whales, these marvelous creatures are no more than floating raw material for a number of products. A large whale is a prize package worth between ten and thirty thousand dollars. The whalers haul it aboard a factory ship where it is cut in small pieces. Its bones and fat are boiled to extract a great quantity of oil. The meat is frozen, some of it for humans to eat but much of it to make dog food and rations for ranch mink. Much whale oil is made into margarine, or into cosmetics, shoe polish, paint, and soap. All of these products can be made from other kinds of oil.

As the whales have grown scarcer, one country after another has given up hunting them. Now only the Japanese and the Russians go on. For a long time few people knew or cared what was happening to the whales, but in the past few years many people have learned about it. Conservationists have become more and more filled with sorrow and anger over this unnecessary slaughter. They are trying to find a way to persuade the Russians and the Japanese to stop killing whales.

To people who love animals it seems terribly wrong to kill these great, sensitive, intelligent creatures for any purpose. As more and more people learn more about whales they realize that they are also precious to us alive in the sea. If enough people protest against the killing of whales it is possible that it can be stopped. Already there are many, many of us who pray that day will come soon.

For Further Reading

Alpers, Antony. 1961. *Dolphins: The Myth and the Mammal.* Boston: Houghton Mifflin Co. *Also* New York: Penguin Books, Inc.

Caldwell, David K., and Melba C. 1972. *The World of the Bottlenosed Dolphin.* Philadelphia: J. B. Lippincott Co.

Cousteau, Jacques-Yves, and Diolé, Philippe. 1972. *The Whale: Mighty Monarch of the Sea.* Garden City, N.Y.: Doubleday & Co., Inc.

Friends of the Earth. 1972. *Whale Campaign Manual.* San Francisco: Friends of the Earth.

Gaskin, D. E. 1973. *Whales, Dolphins, and Seals.* New York: St. Martin's Press, Inc.

Kellogg, Winthrop N. 1961. *Porpoises and Sonar.* Chicago: University of Chicago Press.

McIntyre, Joan, ed. 1974. *Mind in the Waters.* New York: Charles Scribner's Sons; San Francisco: Sierra Club.

McNulty, Faith. 1974. *The Great Whales.* Garden City, N.Y.: Doubleday & Co., Inc.

Matthews, Leonard Harrison, ed. 1968. *The Whale.* New York: Simon & Schuster, Inc.

Mowat, Farley. 1972. *A Whale for the Killing.* Boston: Little, Brown & Co.

Norris, Kenneth S., ed. 1966. *Whales, Dolphins and Porpoises.* Berkeley: University of California Press.

Robertson, R. B. 1954. *Of Whales and Men.* New York: Alfred A. Knopf, Inc.

Scheffer, Victor B. 1969. *The Year of the Whale.* New York: Charles Scribner's Sons.

Slijper, E. J. 1962. *Whales.* New York: Basic Books, Inc.

Stenuit, Robert. 1968. *The Dolphin, Cousin to Man.* New York: Sterling Publishing Co., Inc. *Also* 1972. Osborne, Catherine, tr. New York: Bantam Books, Inc.

Tomilin, A. G. 1967. *Mammals of the U.S.S.R. and Adjacent Countries,* vol. 9. Published for the Smithsonian Institution and the National Science Foundation, Washington, D.C., by the Israel Program for Scientific Translations. Available from the U.S. Department of Commerce, Clearinghouse for Federal Scientific and Technical Information, Springfield, Va. 22151.

Index

The word *whale* refers here to whales and dolphins collectively, except in reference to particular species.

87

Format by Gloria Bressler
Set in 12 pt. Caledonia
Composed by Haddon Craftsmen
Printed by The Murray Printing Company
Bound by Haddon Craftsmen
HARPER & ROW, PUBLISHERS, INCORPORATED